Grain Free Cookbook:

Grain Free Recipes For Better Health

By

Valerie Alston

Table of Contents

Introduction 5

Chapter 1. Breakfast Recipes 7

    Baked Bacon, Eggs and Greens in Hollandaise Sauce 7

    Sweet and Smokey Hash 9

    Ham and Cheese Baked Omelette 10

    Making Your Own Granola 11

    Make Your Own Coffee Creamer 13

    Eggs Benedict for Breakfast 14

Chapter 2. Lunch and Dinner Recipes 15

    "Look Ma, No Tomatoes!" Spaghetti Sauce 15

    All Meat Pizza 18

    Chicken Burgers Made Extra Hot for Lunch 20

Chapter 3. Dessert Recipes 22

    Oatmeal Cookies 22

    Grain Free Sugary Lemon Bars 24

    Minty and Chocolaty Macaroons 26

Final Words 28

Thank You Page 30

Grain Free Cookbook: Grain Free Recipes For Better Health

By Valerie Alston

© Copyright 2014 Valerie Alston

Reproduction or translation of any part of this work beyond that permitted by section 107 or 108 of the 1976 United States Copyright Act without permission of the copyright owner is unlawful. Requests for permission or further information should be addressed to the author.

This publication is designed to provide accurate and authoritative information in regard to the subject matter covered. This work is sold with the understanding that the publisher is not engaged in rendering legal, accounting, or other professional services. If legal advice or other expert assistance is required, the services of a competent professional person should be sought.

First Published, 2014

Printed in the United States of America

Introduction

Going grain free is what these words exactly mean, eating foods that do not contain grains. Grains could be any kind of food that is made of rice, oats, cornmeal, barley and so much more. The most common grain foods that people eat each day are bread, cereals, pasta and tortillas and adapting a grain free diet plan is eliminating all these food items from your usual meal plan.

Proponents of a grain free diet say that eating grain free meals could be one of the best ways to avoid a lot of gastrointestinal and medical conditions. The reason for this is that most grains contain gluten which is a kind of protein that is the main cause of celiac disease and a sensitive gastrointestinal system. Gluten is one of the hardest proteins to digest and having gluten stay longer in your gut can ultimately lead to a damaged gut, the presence of autoimmune diseases, skin problems and so many more health conditions. Grains also contain phytic acid which is an ant nutrient that is solely found in plants. Phytic acid binds with important nutrients that you get from foods like iron, calcium, magnesium and zinc resulting in nutrient deficiencies and countless medical conditions. There are more reasons why grains should be avoided like the presence of lectin that irritates the gastrointestinal lining and the presence of other ant nutrients like alpha amylase inhibitors as well as protease inhibitors. Anyone that has trouble with digestion and have unresolved medical issues should consider altering his diet to healthier and better grain free meals.

This book has various grain free recipes which will help you to follow the diet.

Chapter 1. Breakfast Recipes

Baked Bacon, Eggs and Greens in Hollandaise Sauce

There are zero grains in this recipe all you get are healthy servings of protein from eggs and bacon and of course your fiber and minerals found in delicious greens. You need about 4 ounces of bacon strips, a cup of mixed greens of your choice (these could be spinach, kale or chards), about 8 large eggs and half a cup of Hollandaise sauce.

Chop the bacon strips into small pieces. Prepare your oven by preheating this to 400 degrees Fahrenheit. Heat a medium-sized skillet and cook the chopped bacon until the fat has drained from the meat and the bacon has started to become crisp. This process should take about 5 to 8 minutes; do not remove from heat. Add the greens and then sauté until all the greens are cooked or wilted.

Use 4 medium sized ovenproof dishes to bake the dish. Place the cooked greens and bacon in each of the dish and then top with two eggs each. Occasionally stick a fork in the oven proof dishes to find out if the dish is cooked; the mixture should not be runny and should not stick to the fork. The dish is ready when this happens. Remove the dishes from the oven and place these on the counter to cool. While these are cooling, drizzle with warm Hollandaise sauce and then serve. This recipe is good for 4 servings. You may add more ingredients if you need to cook for more people.

Sweet and Smokey Hash

Breakfast is the most important meal of the day and this meal supplies you with protein from bacon and eggs and minerals form sweet potatoes. This is very easy to prepare and is considered a complete meal that may be eaten at once. You will need about 6 strips of bacon, 2 medium-sized sweet potatoes, 4 medium-sized eggs, and ½ teaspoon of chili powder, ¼ teaspoon of cayenne powder if you want a hot dish and a teaspoon of sea salt.

Chop the bacon strips into small pieces and then cook in a small skillet on medium heat. Cook the bacon pieces until most of the fat has been removed. Scrub the sweet potatoes very well and cut these into very thin half lengthwise pieces. Add these thin strips in the pan of bacon fat as well as all the seasoning; cook the sweet potatoes until these are tender enough to bite on. When the sweet potato pieces are ready, drain the excess fat from the pan and then crack the eggs into the pan and then cover. Cook the dish for 8 more minutes. The dish is ready when all the egg whites are hard and formed while the yolks remain soft. Serve while the dish is still hot.

Ham and Cheese Baked Omelette

Boring omelette cooked in a pan is a thing of the past with this grain free baked omelette using very simple ingredients. You will need about 8 to 10 medium-sized eggs, a cup of cheddar cheese shredded into small pieces, a ½ cup of almond milk, ½ cup of diced ham, a dash of sea salt and a dash of grated nutmeg.

Prepare your oven; preheat it to about 350 degrees Fahrenheit. Use a baking dish that is 9 inch round or a 1.5 quart dish would do. Lightly grease the pan with butter or you may use coconut oil. In a large mixing bowl, whisk all the eggs along with the almond milk. When the two has been completely mixed, add cheese, ham and all the seasoning. Stir the mixture really well. Place this mixture in the baking dish and then bake until the eggs are cooked. You can tell that the mixture is cooked when the eggs have gone fluffy and turned golden brown.

Making Your Own Granola

What if you do not have time to cook during breakfast? You may try this recipe to make your own healthy, grain free granola breakfast treat. You need about 3 cups of gluten free rolled oats, a cup of chopped almonds, ½ cups of flax seeds, ½ cup of coconut flakes (dried and unsweetened), ¼ cup of palm sugar, ½ tablespoons of cinnamon, ¼ cups of honey (have 2 tablespoons extra just in case), ¼ cup of virgin coconut oil, ¾ teaspoon sea salt, 1 tablespoon of vanilla extract and a cup of raisins (the more the better).

Preheat your oven to 165 degrees Fahrenheit; this is the ideal temperature to just dry the ingredients out. Combine your almonds, flax seeds, coconut, palm sugar, oats and cinnamon; mix these ingredients really well in a large bowl. In a separate small bowl, combine oil, salt, vanilla and honey. Use 2 large sheet pans to dry your ingredients; place parchment paper on the pans. Combine the dry and the wet ingredients together and mix very well. Divide the ingredients into two mixtures and place each on one sheet pan.

Bake these for 250 degrees Fahrenheit for about an hour. You may need to inspect and turn the ingredients to distribute the brown roasted color evenly. As the granola begins to harden, stir in the raisins and then allow to bake completely. When the granola is ready, remove from the oven and then allow to cool on the counter. Chop into small bite sized pieces and eat or you may place in an airtight container to ensure that these will stay fresh and crispy every day.

Make Your Own Coffee Creamer

This is a fructose-free and grain free coffee creamer that you can use every day. You may also want to make some more to store and use during the afternoon. This recipe is good for 2 cups of coffee. You need a cup of almond milk, a cup of coconut milk, 2 tablespoons raw honey, a vanilla bean and about 2 tablespoons of maple syrup.

In a medium-sized saucepan, combine the milk and sweetener and stir over medium heat. Allow to boil and then remove from heat. Prepare the vanilla bean by slicing it in half along its side. Remove the seeds and place the seeds and the bean in milk. Allow this to steep for 30 minutes. After the designated time, remove the seeds and the bean from the milk by straining the milk. Your coffee creamer is ready to use or you may place this in an airtight container and store in the refrigerator for about a week.

Eggs Benedict for Breakfast

Eggs are very important protein source in a grain free diet. The fact that eggs may be turned into different meals and are very easy to cook you will be able to prepare this meal even when you are in a hurry. You will need 4 medium-sized eggs, poached, ½ tablespoon of virgin coconut oil, 2 cups of spinach, about 2 ounces of ham, ½ clove of garlic, crushed, a dash of salt and pepper, optional dinner rolls and a dash of Hollandaise sauce.

In a medium-sized saucepan, sauté spinach, garlic and salt and pepper; when the greens have wilted, remove from the pan and then cook ham and cook for about a minute. Continue cooking if you are preparing uncooked ham; this must be completely cooked on each side. Arrange your breakfast dish this way: place the spinach first, then neatly fold the ham in an exact size of the egg and then place the poached egg on top. Drizzle with Hollandaise sauce and then serve.

Chapter 2. Lunch and Dinner Recipes

"Look Ma, No Tomatoes!" Spaghetti Sauce

This is a recipe that will surprise you. This will match your grain –free spaghetti meal perfectly. Since some people that have sensitive stomachs cannot tolerate grains may not be able to tolerate tomatoes as well. This recipe gives you a chance to enjoy authentic spaghetti flavour without all the stomach cramps and problems with digestion. You may cook this recipe or dinner or lunch but if you wish you may prepare this recipe in advance and keep it in the refrigerator. You will need about 2 tablespoons of unsalted butter, 2 tablespoons of virgin olive oil, 2 cups of medium-size carrots, 2 cups of beets, a cup of diced yellow corn, a stalk of celery, 2 cloves of garlic, 2 large bacon pieces, 2 teaspoons of salt, ¼ teaspoon of freshly cracked black pepper, ½ cup of red wine, a cup of chicken stock, 2 small bay leaves, a tablespoon of fresh basil, a teaspoon of oregano (dried and ground), a teaspoon of thyme, a tablespoon of apple cider vinegar and a pound of ground pork (or if you prefer to use ground beef instead).

Prepare the vegetables; peel and dice the carrots, beets and onions, chop the celery stalks into small pieces, chop the bacon into small pieces and chop the basil into fine pieces. In a large saucepan, melt the butter along with the olive oil and then sauté the onions until these are translucent and flavorful. Add the garlic and cook but be careful not to burn the garlic. Mix in the bacon and cook along with the garlic and onions; cook until the bacon is light and crispy. Place the carrots, celery and beets. Cook these until these are soft and tender. Afterwards add the wine and the chicken stock; simmer and then reduce the heat. Remove from heat and then allow to cool for about 15 minutes and then place in a blender. Pulse the mixture for about 15 seconds then then continue to blend until you have a smooth and even mixture.

When the sauce is ready you may return this to a large saucepan and bring to a boil. Add the spices like the bay leaves, oregano, thyme and basil; add the vinegar and then simmer. Take the ground meat and then crumble this all over the mixture. Cook the ground meat for about 20 to 30 minutes. Stir the mixture constantly to prevent it from sticking at the bottom of the pan. Check on the meat time and again to ensure that it is fully cooked. Cover and reduce heat when the meat is about to cook. The sauce may come out too thick and this may depend on the amount of stock that you put in the sauce. You may adjust this if you want a lighter sauce or if you would like a thicker sauce you may want to use a little less chicken stock at the beginning of the recipe. You may add this to your favourite grain free spaghetti noodles, just remember to cook your noodles according to package instructions. Simply add this no-tomato spaghetti sauce over cooked pasta or if you prefer to use it next time, place it in a covered container and then refrigerate.

All Meat Pizza

This is an all meat pizza delight that you can serve for lunch, dinner and even for a snack. Almost everyone loves pizza and this dish will surely be a welcome treat during weekends with the whole family. Remember that buying ready-to-use pizza crust from the supermarket does not guarantee that you are using grain free pizza crust. Therefore you need to make one. You need these ingredients to make the crust: ¾ cup of raw cashews, 3 tablespoons of almond flour, ¼ cup of coconut flour, ½ teaspoon of baking soda, a dash of salt, a dash of garlic granules, 2 medium-sized eggs, 2 tablespoons of milk, ½ tablespoon of sugar, ½ teaspoon of apple cider vinegar, 2 tablespoons of extra virgin olive oil, a tablespoon of cold water, fresh parsley finely chopped and 2 tablespoons of fresh basil leaves freshly chopped too.

For the pizza ingredients you will need a cup of marinara sauce, ¾ cups of raw mozzarella cheese, and 1 cup of salami without casing and sliced thinly, 2 pieces of bacon, ¼ cup of mushrooms and ¼ cup of black olives.

Prepare your oven by preheating it to 350 degrees Fahrenheit. Shred the cheese, slice the salami, cook and then chop the bacon into smaller pieces, pit the black olives and then slice into small pieces. Use a food processor to process the almonds into almond flour. When the almond flour is ready, add the baking soda, coconut flour, salt and the garlic. Process these ingredients for about a minute. Then add the eggs, apple cider vinegar, almond milk, oil and water. Process for another minute and then scrape the sides. By now you have small pizza dough with a smooth consistency. Add the chopped parsley and basil leaves and then process again for a few seconds. Remove from the processor and allow to rest for a couple of minutes. Get two pieces of parchment paper. Place one parchment paper on the counter and then place the dough on top. Add a few sprinkles of flour and then place the remaining parchment paper on top. Use a rolling pin, bottle or your hands to transform the ball into a flattened disc. Roll the dough until you have a circle that is ¼ inch thick. Bake the crust in your oven for about 12 minutes and then take this out of the oven. Place marinara sauce, cheese salami and meat over the sauce. Lastly place the mushrooms and olives. When you are done, place the pizza back in the oven to bake for another 15 minutes. The pizza is done when the cheese turns golden brown; use a large sharp knife to cut the pizza into smaller slices.

Chicken Burgers Made Extra Hot for Lunch

This is a chili chicken burger that uses grain free rolls and not ordinary hamburger buns. You will need the following for the patties recipe: A pound of ground chicken, about ¼ cup of red onions, ¼ cup of red bell peppers, a small clove of garlic, a tablespoon of cilantro, a dash of salt and pepper and ¼ cup of freshly-squeezed lime juice.

Instead of ordinary bread, you also need dinner rolls grain free, a cup of guacamole, 3 to 4 pieces of Romaine lettuce, a large sandwich tomato sliced into large pieces, 2 tablespoons of homemade fat-free mayonnaise and 4 slices of grass fed cheese.

First you will need to prepare all the vegetables needed for the patties. Chop vegetables into small pieces or use a food processor to ensure that these are minced evenly. In a medium-sized pan, sauté the onions, bell peppers and the cloves of garlic in olive oil in medium heat. Cook these veggies until these are soft and aromatic.

Place the chicken meat, onion and all the spices and all the flavorings in a medium-sized bowl. Mix all the ingredients with a spatula or you may also use your hands to mix evenly. This recipe will make about 4 large patties so divide the mixture into 4 and then make large patties with each using your hands. Prepare your grill and then when it is hot, grill the chicken burger patty for 6 minutes on each side. Toast the dinner rolls for a nice and hot sandwich and then create your hamburger with the rest of the ingredients.

Chapter 3. Dessert Recipes

Oatmeal Cookies

This is a totally new way to make your favourite oatmeal cookies. This is a grain free recipe so take note of the many changes from your usual oatmeal cookies recipe. You will need ¼ cups of palm shortening, a large egg placed in room temperature, ½ cup of raw honey, a teaspoon of vanilla extract, 4 teaspoons of cinnamon, ¾ teaspoons of nutmeg, a cup of blanched almond flour, 2 tablespoons of coconut flour, ½ teaspoons of baking soda, a dash of sea salt, 2 teaspoons of flax seeds finely ground, ¾ cup of coconut, dried and finely shredded and a cup of raisins.

Preheat your oven to about 350 degrees and then with the use of a stand mixer prepare the other ingredients. Place the shortening and the eggs in the mixer and then mix for about a minute. You may also use a hand held electric mixer. When you are done, add the vanilla and the honey. Mix these until these have turned creamy. In a small bowl, mix the cinnamon, baking soda, flours, flax seeds and the nutmeg. Add the dry ingredients to the wet ingredients until these have been completely combined. Mix these ingredients but pause periodically to scrape the ingredients that are placed along the sides of the bowl. Mix for about a minute. Finally, add the coconut and the raisins and then mix for another 30 seconds.

Prepare a cookie sheet by lining these with parchment paper. Use an ice cream scooper to scoop a cookie mixture and then place these on the parchment paper. Press on the center of the ball to make the balls into cookies. Place the cookie sheet in the oven and then bake these for about 10 to 15 minutes. The edges of the cookies should be slightly browned to signal that the cookies are cooked. Place the cookies in a wire rack before eating. Make sure that the cookies are cool if you want to store these in an airtight container or plastic.

Grain Free Sugary Lemon Bars

These lemon bars are perfect for a snack but are as healthy since these are grain free. You will need about ½ cup of finely ground sunflower seeds, 2/3 cup of coconut flour, 1/3 teaspoon on baking soda, 2 tablespoons of coconut oil or unsalted butter, 2 tablespoons of honey, 2 medium-sized eggs, a teaspoon of vanilla extract and a teaspoon of freshly squeezed lemon juice. For the lemon bar filling you will need 3 large-sized eggs and 1 egg yolk, ½ cup of honey, ¾ cup of fresh lemon juice, 3 tablespoons of coconut flour and a teaspoon of finely grated lemon zest.

Preheat your oven to 350 degrees Fahrenheit. Combine the ingredients for the crust and place these in a food processor. Mix all these completely and stop to scrape the sides of the bowl until you have smooth dough. You will need a 9x 9 square baking pans, grease this with butter. Place the dough in the pan and make sure that the mixture is equally distributed. You may need to press the dough to the bottom and to the sides to make sure that you have perfect sides of your lemon bar. Place this in the oven and then bake for 10 minutes. Afterwards, remove from the oven and then let it cool on the counter. Combine all the filling ingredients and then allow the flour to stand for about 10 minutes before you continue stirring. Place the filling on top of the baked crust and then place it back in the oven to bake for another 10 to 15 minutes. After baking, cool and then cut into small bars.

Minty and Chocolaty Macaroons

Even when you are not allowed to eat grains you can still enjoy delicious pastries like macaroons and now you can even have them in mint and chocolate varieties. You will need 3 cups of coconut, dried and shredded, ½ cup of cacao powder, ½ cup of raw honey, ½ cup of coconut milk. ½ teaspoon of peppermint extract, ¼ teaspoon of vanilla extract, 1 egg white separated from the yolk and a dash of salt.

Preheat your oven to 325 degrees Fahrenheit. In a large mixing bowl, combine the first six ingredients in a bowl. In a separate bowl and with a stand mixer or a hand mixer beat the egg white and a dash of salt. Continue beating until you can see soft white peaks forming. Add and fold the egg white and salt mixture in the coconut; mix this until these are completely combined. With a tablespoon, scoop out a small amount of dough and then place it on a cookie tray lined with parchment paper. Place in the oven and then bake for at least 30 minutes. Keep a watchful eye on your macaroons by turning the pan about. After the time is up, place the finished macaroons in a cooling rack. You may also dip the macaroons in melted chocolate, preferably dark chocolate and then allow to set in the refrigerator. Place in a container or a box when the macaroons are completely cool. Should you would like to bake more macaroons then you may do so by increasing the amount of ingredients that are provided. If you also find the recipe sweet, reduce the amount of honey or for a sweeter batch of macaroons, try adding or doubling the amount of honey in the recipe.

Final Words

As you can see, grain free meals are no different from the usual foods that you eat and your favourite foods. You can still enjoy cooking, baking and eating the foods that you usually enjoy like hamburgers, cookies, desserts and treats but of course these are prepared without using a tinge of grain. When it comes to taste, there is not much difference in eating foods that are prepared grain free the only concern is preparing dishes with extra effort since you may need to look for these ingredients carefully in markets, stores and in supermarkets.

Going grain free may be introduced also to your family other than indulging in eating this kind of meal alone. When you include your family in selecting and eating foods that are grain free you will find it easier to eat these meals since you do not need to prepare an extra meal for yourself. Parents may start a grain free eating habit in your child to be able to take advantage of the many health-giving advantages of this diet. You can start today and indulge your entire family to a grain free breakfast, lunch, dinner and even desserts; you will find that they will never even know the difference in the meals that you serve. Going grain free is not just a recipe or a meal, it is a lifestyle. You should also limit eating outdoors or eating in fast food chains since you are not completely aware of the foods that you are eating as well as the foods that are served. So be a smart consumer and learn how to prepare, cook and eat grain free.

Thank You Page

I want to personally thank you for reading my book. I hope you found information in this book useful and I would be very grateful if you could leave your honest review about this book. I certainly want to thank you in advance for doing this.

www.ingramcontent.com/pod-product-compliance
Lightning Source LLC
LaVergne TN
LVHW021746060526
838200LV00052B/3513